JEFF GNASS
IDAHO
MAGNIFICENT WILDERNESS

PHOTOGRAPHY BY JEFF GNASS

WESTCLIFFE PUBLISHERS, INC. ENGLEWOOD, COLORADO

CONTENTS

International Standard
   Book Number: *ISBN 0-942394-86-0*

Library of Congress
   Catalogue Card Number: *88-51244*

Copyright, Photographs
   and Text: *Jeff Gnass, 1989*

Editor: *John Fielder*

Assistant Editor: *Margaret Terrell Morse*

Production Manager: *Mary Jo Lawrence*

Typographer: *Dianne J. Borneman*

Printed in Japan by   *Dai Nippon Printing*
                           Company, Ltd., Tokyo

Published by   *Westcliffe Publishers, Inc.*
                           2650 South Zuni Street
                           Englewood, Colorado 80110

Bibliography

1. Davis, Nelle Portrey. *Stump Ranch Pioneer.* New York: Dodd, Mead & Company, Inc., 1942. Reprinted by permission of the publisher.
2. Quotations from *Idaho: A Guide in Word and Picture* by The Idaho Writers' Project are copyright 1937, 1950, 1964, 1977 by Oxford University Press, Inc., and reprinted with their permission.
3. Irving, Washington. *A Tour on the Prairies.* New York: Pantheon Books, a division of Random House, Inc., 1967. From *The Works of Washington Irving* (Kinderhook Edition, 1864).
4. Peterson, F. Ross. *Idaho, A Bicentennial History.* New York: W.W. Norton & Company, Inc., 1976. Reprinted by permission of the publisher.

First Frontispiece: *Whitebark pine and Mount Regan overlook Sawtooth Lake, Sawtooth Wilderness*

Second Frontispiece: *Aspen take on unusual autumn colors at City of Rocks, Albion Mountains*

Third Frontispiece: *Mule's ears wildflowers and grasses explode in spring celebration, South Fork Boise River Canyon*

Title Page: *Sunset clouds soar above Devils Bedstead, Pioneer Mountains*

Right: *Monkeyflowers and native plants flourish in Cayuse Creek Canyon, Bitterroot Mountains*

FOREWORD

Chance placed me in Idaho while growing up, and uncertainty brought me back after college. But at some point intention took over, and I realized I would be staying. The places you see in this book, and others like them, are the reason why.

Living in Idaho exacts a price, measured not in dollars but in isolation and inertia. But I have found no price tag yet for the opportunity to spend time in Idaho's wild places. There are so many, and each holds so much.

Take a look at Jeff Gnass's images of Priest Lake, for instance. When I was last there the lake was frozen, snow was falling and the great sweep east up to the Selkirk Crest was lost in cloud. I stood where Granite Creek tumbled a black wedge of water into the ice. As I walked toward Bartoo Island, strange booms and scrapes beneath the ice seemed the only sounds in the world. After the plowing stopped at Indian Creek, I skied a white lane between blurred dark woods to Huckleberry Bay. Alone, wary, wrapped by weather in a small, still world, I felt nearer to my surroundings than I had ever been when able to see them.

White-tailed deer were nearby, wintering on the lakeshore. Grizzly bears slept in dens above my trail. Mountain caribou were moving up through 10 feet of snow near the Selkirk Crest, where they would feed till spring on lichen strung from branches only squirrels could reach in summer. The area's few wolves — were they here or across the border in Canada? Around me too were cougar, moose, elk, mountain goat, black bear. In this remote northern corner of Idaho, a diversity of wildlife are drawn to its mix of lush habitats.

I skied on, tips aimed north. A mile above me and six miles farther on, over the crest, lay the head of Long Canyon, Idaho's rainforest remnant and the last wholly roadless drainage in the American Selkirks. That green cathedral of great cedars, hemlocks and white pine,

where even the rocks, even the water is green, was now encased in winter. Was snow penetrating the thick forest cover like sunlight in summer, in narrow white shafts here and there?

Another, very different forest lies 700 miles southeast of where I stood, on a desert in eastern Idaho. Craters of the Moon National Monument marks the northern edge of a million acres of lava and ash, a violent, waterless scatter of flows, cracks, caves, tubes, cones and craters. Most of the monument has never felt a human foot. But bring water, and you can walk the longest, deepest rift in North America's skin. Here you will find kipukas — inland islands ringed by lava, with lone juniper trees older than Long Canyon's cedars.

Here too is Big Southern Butte, which rides these volcanics like a huge ship from whose deck all is before you. Water was on my mind when I climbed the butte, and I pondered how this dry, empty, exposed land seems to demand a spare and distant eye. Then, to my surprise, I rounded a slight bend and walked into a forest.

The way to appreciate what trees create in a forest is to stumble on the only example for miles around. Shade. Places to lie down. The interplay of branches and leaves. Sanctuary for birds.

I stopped, and began to learn what many images in this book confirm — the spare and distant desert is unpredictable.

It is pure historical accident that Idaho holds places so different and so far apart as Priest Lake and Craters of the Moon. Idahoans, especially northern Idahoans, who contend with other results of our peculiar boundaries — in transport, time zones and politics — regularly damn the accident. You will see in these pages why I'm so grateful for it.

History aside, there is a heart to Idaho that belongs nowhere else, nor could it. Idaho has more wild land

Little penstemons bloom below pinnacles in the
Sawtooth Range, Sawtooth Wilderness

than any state south of Alaska — some 18 million acres. Most of it, and so most of the images in this book, is in central Idaho — the entire length of the Salmon and Clearwater rivers, plus the backing headwaters of the St. Joe, Payette, Boise, Wood and Lost rivers. These mountain waters and wild areas bind north to south.

The Salmon and Clearwater river basins are shaped much like the strands of DNA in our cells. The streams curl and fold around and upon themselves; stretched out they would circle the earth. Long ago, this vast intricacy was settled by two fish — the salmon and the steelhead trout. These ocean-going fish are born in mountain streams 800 miles or more inland. Heading downriver, they pass through the Snake and Columbia rivers and on into the Pacific. After years of ranging the northern ocean, they return as big strong fish to fight their way upriver to their streams of birth. They spawn the next generation and die.

Much makes these fish compelling. The great circle of their lives. Their ferocious tenacity. The roots they sink in human lives — in communities, economies, hearts. Given clean streams and clear paths, they teem in our waters.

Watch a salmon push up the Salmon River — or later bleach and die in a headwater creek — while thinking what it has done to get there. Each fish embodies and unforgettably teaches relation, connection, the web of life. We have yet to learn this teaching, as wild salmon and steelhead are now endangered in central Idaho, their circle shredded by dams, mud, nets. But if we learn it, far more than a future for Idaho fish will follow.

Idahoans remain at cross-purposes about the natural areas highlighted in this book. Wilderness has defined us to ourselves, even as this frontier, with its freedoms and hazards, has steadily receded elsewhere. Yet we too have progressively reclaimed, roaded and developed it. In the next decade this same fate is slated for the Payette Crest, the Owyhee Platea, Priest Lake

and much of the country around the Clearwater River.

Today, and surely tomorrow, the future of these areas arouses fierce public debate, with sturdy forces on each side. It's clear which side I'm on. I hope you, after seeing these photographs, will come to agree and help.

Why? Take a look at Jeff Gnass's image of Castle Peak, which stands sentinel over the largest unprotected wild area left in the national forests of the West. In 1987 I stood where Gnass stood. As I descended, mountain goats were feeding down the ridge to my left. I walked beside the lovely lakes at the foot of the peak, and the next day walked up and over to the meadows and lakes on the back side. Throughout the trip I couldn't take my eyes off that mountain. A month later I found a motto, from Robert Frost, for the place and the excesses of feeling it stirred in me: "May something go always unharvested! / May much stay out of our stated plan."

In 1978 I asked the best man I've ever known, outdoor writer Ted Trueblood, what there was in wilderness that made him work so hard for decades to preserve it. He closed his eyes and tried. Finally he gave up — "It's just *good*. I like it." — and began describing the elk in autumn in his favorite basin. He could bring a place alive with words, but why he went and what he felt was hard to say, perhaps better not said. Words can't contain it. Even camera images cannot.

Why go to these places, and why should they remain if no one ever goes again? We can stack and weigh the sensible reasons — economic, social, scientific, they matter more each year. But the real reason is there at Chamberlain Divide: Castle Peak, uncalculated, prodigal, uncontained. And there in Chamberlain Creek: salmon, rivetted to their immeasurable, unharvested ways. May they always remain.

— PAT FORD

Cattails and hare tracks on lake snow, Bear Lake National Wildlife Refuge

PREFACE

Of all the western states, Idaho easily epitomizes the rural West of today. It just as readily offers a nostalgic glimpse, through rustic ranches and roadside communities, of a West long passed. With the milestone of its statehood centennial, Idaho can also gaze back at its rich history from the vantage point of hi-tech farms and bustling cities.

Early frontiersmen dared to explore this territory of bountiful game, mineral-rich mountains, virgin forests and sweeping rangelands. Idaho's rugged geography was not easily settled. The Gem State is the most mountainous of all Rocky Mountain states, boasting more than 80 ranges recognized by map names. Many more mingle so effectively with their neighbors that the namers haven't found them.

Idaho's Panhandle hosts a number of low mountain ranges, including the southern extent of one often thought to be entirely Canadian — the Selkirks. A mild maritime-like climate nurtures lush forests and dense vegetation in this region. Capacious valleys scraped out during past ice ages now harbor lakes that fill the deepest trenches of these U-shaped glacial canyons. Lake Pend Oreille, Idaho's largest, forms a deep, blue pool at the southern end of the Purcell Trench.

Central Idaho is largely defined by the Idaho Batholith, a massive swell of sporadically exposed granite that nudges up against Montana along the crest of the Bitterroots. A view across these mountains reveals a sea of timbered ridges and plunging valleys, deeply cut by the network of streams and rivers. With few roads penetrating this rugged country, this is the nucleus of Idaho's wilderness. Travel through most parts is still by foot or horseback, or by water down such courses as the Salmon and the Selway rivers.

No doubt the most majestic mountain scenery in Idaho is the Sawtooth Range, a complex of spiny alpine ridges that crisscrosses at magnificent jagged peaks. This range supports an abundance of jewel-like lakes tucked away in cirques or secluded in the forest-covered hills of ancient glacial moraines.

To the east of the Sawtooths lies a region of drier ranges and broad valleys. Places with names like *Lemhi, Lost River* and *Pahsimeroi* are to the history of the open range as wool and rawhide are to its essence. Sagebrush and grasslands dominate in these mountains. Near the summits, few trees cling to the arid ridges. In the canyons and lower elevations, range cattle interrupt the view more often than elk and pronghorn.

Farther south, Idaho's central ranges shrink to rounded ridges and foothills, giving way to the great lava flows that fan out across the Snake River Plain. This vast expanse is occasionally ruffled by low hills, dotted with cinder buttes and pockmarked by craters. It stretches south toward mountains of the Basin and Range province that reach across the Utah/Nevada border and east toward the gas- and oil-rich uplifts of the Overthrust Belt formed along the Wyoming border.

To the southwest the Snake River Plain runs up against the Owyhee Plateau, a great uplift stretching out below the Owyhee Mountains. Water courses like Big Jack's Creek and the Bruneau River, flowing from these lesser-known mountains, have cut through the basalt veneer to form intricate canyon systems.

The borders that now define Idaho were literally formed of what remained after neighboring territories summed up their own perimeters. But a portion of Idaho's border with Oregon was declared by a geological course of action more than a historical one. Near the western edge of the state, the Snake River turns and flows north, where it has cut through metamorphic remnants and created Hells Canyon, the deepest gorge in North America. Sitting above Hells Canyon to the east, the glacial-contoured Seven Devils Mountains rise to imposing basalt peaks.

When I began photographing this book three summers ago, I looked forward with delight to the thought of spending a couple of years exploring new alpine terrain, resplendent wildflower meadows and autumns of fall foliage. I couldn't have imagined three successive drought years would lie ahead, and the effect

Sunset casts its spell on Grays Lake and Caribou Mountain, Grays Lake National Wildlife Refuge

this lack of moisture would have on the features of the landscape. The drought notwithstanding, I experienced a great deal of Idaho's natural beauty and found a much more diverse landscape than I had originally predicted. With this portfolio, I've aimed to create as faithful a record as possible of my glimpses of Idaho in hopes I might share these impressions.

My focus when photographing Idaho was on wilderness, in any form it was manifest. I made more than a dozen extended trips for this project. Frequently it was necessary to visit an area several times before I found the exact lighting qualities or seasonal highlights I was looking for. And sometimes it never happened. I have no photographic record of some of the places I visited.

But every trip resulted in memorable experiences. Sometimes it was the luck of being at the right place at the right time. At other times I had the fortune to discover distinctive images when going out in bad weather to explore with my camera.

One sunset I was photographing on a stark granite ridge in an area of the Great Burn in the Bitterroot Range. I couldn't help but draw analogies between the scenery around me and the Yellowstone fires that were raging out of control. With a 360-degree panorama of the surrounding area, I noticed how naked forest relics stood out on distant slopes and ridges. The Great Burn fire occurred 78 years ago. Mentally I tried to superimpose this austere image on the Yellowstone landscape of the future and wondered if its dense stands of lodgepole would ever be fully reforested in my lifetime. It was disturbing to realize that the fires that were consuming Yellowstone were, to some degree or other, a consequence of man's meddling in the natural affairs of the forest over the past 100 years. As I worked my way in the creeping darkness along the blocky ridge toward camp, a chilling wind picked up and the stars started coming out one by one. When I walked into camp an hour later I glanced up at the blazing night sky and realized how much we have yet to learn about our planet.

While searching out images for this book, I was dismayed to notice how many additions there were to the quilt-like logging scars that have spread over the mountains in such a relatively short period. This reinforced to me the urgency of maintaining the few unspoiled areas that remain — areas that must be off limits to man's usual tinkering with the natural order of things. These are places where we should be forever only visitors. Wild biosystems are essential references for measuring how much we are in or out of balance with the planet. We need areas set aside where we can go and compare ourselves with the raw spirit of a wild land. Even if we never visit these places, we still need to know they are there.

Outside of Alaska, Idaho contains some of the largest federally protected wilderness areas in the country. Idaho also has some of the largest remaining roadless areas in the lower 48 states. A movement has been underway for several years for new laws that would accord formal wilderness status to these areas. While following the struggle by environmentalists toward this end, I was dismayed at how provincial the attitudes of congressmen and special interest groups were toward the land. It is sad to realize they would plunder these last unspoiled areas for the chance at a few more board feet of timber or troy ounces of ore. Wherever these lands are located, they belong to all people.

With so many areas that face chronic development, we must be ever diligent in our efforts to save the few unspoiled areas. Attacks on these lands will continue to mount as demands for natural resources grow and population increases — demands that can be largely met through less extravagant consumption. As we pollute the air and water and adopt less-caring attitudes toward the land through our actions, we must realize that we already are suffering the consequences of our mishandling of the environment — a destruction to be the legacy of future generations.

I hope that the photographs in this book will not only offer a glimpse of wilderness, one that is still an intrinsic part of Idaho, but that they will also foster the realization that wilderness is an inseparable part of the human spirit.

— JEFF GNASS

On the brink of Upper Mesa Falls on the Henry's Fork,
Targhee National Forest

COLOR

The chromatic diversity in nature is as varied as our imaginations. Color is the component least under my control when photographing the landscape. But color can be manifest another way — in the character of light. I favor the chromatic qualities that occur during the period I refer to as the "edge of day." Twilight, with its subtle, moody hues, can make an ethereal expression about the landscape, one that can be as emotionally powerful as dazzling color.

Left: *Red and yellow lichens grow in curious patterns on welded tuff, Black Canyon in the Mount Bennett Hills*

Above: *River rocks complement autumn reflections on the North Fork Payette River, Salmon River Mountains*

Overleaf: *Riot of spring wildflowers in a pine forest on the Weippe Prairie, Clearwater Mountains*

Upland grasses and hills in the
Pahsimeroi Mountains, Lost River Range

Autumn snow dusts a larch and fir forest,
Bitterroot Range

"A gallop across the prairies in pursuit of game is by no
means so smooth a career as those may imagine who have
only the idea of an open level plain. It is true, the prairies
of the hunting-ground are not so much entangled with
flowering plants and long herbage as the lower prairies, and
are principally covered with short buffalo-grass; but they are
diversified by hill and dale, and where most level, are apt
to be cut up by deep rifts and ravines, . . ."
— *Washington Irving, 1832*

Sagebrush and snow blanket hills, Boulder Mountains

Forested ridges and afternoon shadows in Kelly Creek Canyon, Bitterroot Range

Overleaf: *Naked Great Burn remnants and granite blocks at sunset, Bitterroot Range*

"Annually the dread and danger of forest fires are with us. . . . Mighty green-clad mountains swept in a single evening by a sea of flame! Broad and fertile valleys laid waste by the red demon! 'Crown fires' sweeping through the forests a hundred feet above the ground, blazes leaping from tree to tree, and hurling flaming brands for hundreds of yards, to start new fires wherever they fall! It is a sight to strike terror to the stoutest heart." — *Nelle Portrey Davis, 1942*

*Autumn arrangement of dogbane and granite
boulders, South Fork Clearwater River Canyon,
Clearwater Mountains*

*Cattails grow in backwaters of the Salmon River,
Round Valley near Challis*

". . . this alpine region and the southern steppe are sharp
and complete in their contrast. One is a black and gray area
of impregnable stone. The other is a region of tumultuous
rivers and tiny sheltered basins, of a vast rolling acreage of
high meadows and forested canyons and white zeniths."
— *Idaho Writers' Project, 1950*

---

*Clouds glow as sunset fades on Mount Heyburn in
the Sawtooth Range, Sawtooth Wilderness*

New growth of fir boughs, Bitterroot Range

" . . . the evergreen forest [rose] in a mighty wall of living
grace; and beyond, glimpsed through and above the tree-
tops, were the brooding mountains, blue and somber,
majestic and mighty, and somehow vastly comforting and
reassuring." — *Nelle Portrey Davis, 1942*

FORM

The persistent, searching eye can linger on an endless variety of form and pattern in nature. For me, this means discovery. Seeking out the subject. Locating a model specimen. Finding a distinctive rock formation with an imposing shape or a graphic arrangement of wildflowers, each petal in prime condition. Whether it's a study of striking form or rhythmic pattern, there's always a feeling of excitement when I'm able to turn my attention and the camera to these phrases of nature.

Left: *Western red cedars succumb to age in the Lochsa River Canyon, Bitterroot Range*

Above: *Cirrus clouds and daybreak reflections on Twin Lakes, Payette Crest area in the Salmon River Mountains*

Waterfall on Cow Creek, Selkirk Mountains,
Kaniksu National Forest

Wind-wrinkled sand patterns,
Bruneau Dunes State Park

Overleaf: Frost-covered firs create winter designs,
Pioneer Mountains

"Idaho has huge semi-arid reaches, but it also probably has
more running water than any other State. It has flat
formidable tablelands that defeat everything but sagebrush
and coyote, but it also has more lakes than have ever been
counted and nobody quite knows how many remain
undiscovered and unexplored." — *Idaho Writers' Project, 1950*

Evening twilight settles over Bartoo Island and
Priest Lake, Selkirk Mountains

Douglas fir frames Priest Lake below sunset clouds,
Selkirk Mountains

"Here, in the upper Panhandle, is an area of surpassingly
lovely lakes and of great evergreen forests, . . . This area,
seen from the air, is one of rivers and mountain streams, of
almost countless lakes, and of great dark blankets of forest."
— *Idaho Writers' Project, 1950*

An alpine forest struggles at treeline on a ridge before
Fenn Mountain and the Selway Crags,
Selway-Bitterroot Wilderness

Decaying lodgepole pines in a sunset sky,
Henry's Lake Mountains

Overleaf: Aspen change season below granite
formations at City of Rocks, Albion Mountains

". . . they find this region awful in its aloofness and
inexplicable in its calm. There is no shadow in its bald glare
and no witchery in its horizons: it is candid in sunlight and
alien and ageless in its mood." — *Idaho Writers' Project, 1950*

Sunset pastels tint a weathered whitebark pine,
Lost River Range

Beargrass on Scotchman's Peak overlooks
Lake Pend Oreille at sunset, Cabinet Mountains

"A strange tree, and one of the most unconquerable of alpine
conifers, is the white bark pine which occurs only in the
north . . . at high altitudes, often rimming the world and
often getting flattened into a mass of boughs and ice; and
even at lower levels mountaineers sometimes build their
beds on the wide flat branches lying on the earth. At their
topmost elevations these hardy trees are dwarfed and beaten
down but seldom killed and they often look like young trees
when in fact they are remarkably old."
— *Idaho Writers' Project, 1950*

MOMENT

Moment in landscape photography represents those fleeting events that cannot be predicted or counted on to repeat. In the course of a day, light and atmospheric conditions change from one phase to the next. Dawn becomes daylight. Blue sky turns to cumuli. Showers fade to moonlight. These are somewhat predictable events. But there is another measure of moment in the landscape, such as when snow patches fade to heather, a meadow blushes in flower or trees dress for autumn. While pursuing the sun on its daily trek, I also try to maintain my sensitivity to these seasonal events in nature.

Left: *Limber pine relic stands before sunset clouds, Craters of the Moon National Monument*

Above: *Aspen and afternoon shadows harmonize with autumn, Boulder Mountains*

*Moon and early dawn clouds mingle over the
Sawtooth Range, Sawtooth Wilderness*

*Anemones bloom beside Bernard Lake,
Seven Devils Mountains, Hells Canyon Wilderness*

"And in the west, more remotely, far over the arid steppe
which water will never reclaim, is the magnificent Sawtooth
Range. Here are peaks reaching altitudes of more than 12,000
feet, among which are many tiny valleys, some holding lakes,
some fertile, tilled basins, and all of them walled in by the
forested slopes of other ranges." — *Idaho Writers' Project, 1950*

Frozen cattails emerge from lake snow at sunset,
Bear Lake National Wildlife Refuge

Chimney Rock blushes at sunset, Selkirk Mountains

"Within southern caves in January wild animals may lie
indolently fat in warm chambers; and in the same hour
mountain goats, standing upon the great watersheds, look
across deserts of snow that have completely buried
evergreens thirty feet in height." — *Idaho Writers' Project, 1950*

Foggy sunrise silhouettes poplars,
Coeur d'Alene River Wildlife Area

Sunset sky above a forest skyline,
Bitterroot Range

"I walked briskly but quietly on the carpet, inches deep, of evergreen needles. . . . A startled grouse whirred its way into a cedar thicket. I saw numerous lady-slippers and trillium. The perennial dusk of the deep woods prevailed. The narrow canopy of the blue above was patterned delicately by the needled branches of the evergreens, which nearly met over the road." — *Nelle Portrey Davis, 1942*

Dissipating clouds veil She Devil and He Devil above
Basin Lake, Seven Devils Mountains,
Hells Canyon Wilderness

Granite ramp below the Payette Crest reddens at
sunset, Salmon River Mountains

Overleaf: *Mount Heyburn and the Sawtooth Range*
reflect in Little Redfish Lake at sunrise,
Sawtooth National Recreation Area

"Bounded on the west by the wild Seven Devils area . . . At no point does this elevation fall below 4000 feet, and in most of it the altitude is considerably more than a mile. . . . The underlying formation, dating from the Pre-Cambrian to the Mississippian ages, is granite overlaid by sedimentary beds, folded and eroded. . . . The eroded alluvial deposits have left high, level terraces of sand and gravel." — *Idaho Writers' Project, 1950*

Ice formations and snowfall at Fall Creek Falls,
Caribou Mountains

*Larches and cottonwoods glow in morning sun along
Little Goose Creek, Salmon River Mountains*

"The larch . . . is unlike any other conifer in having almost
no foliage after it reaches some size and in dropping its
leaves when winter comes. A mature tree has in summertime
a bushy top high in the air and a mighty spire of trunk as
straight as a lodgepole. . . . It is this tree that gives the
park-like grandeur of ancient estates to the forest in which
it is found. Limned against light, its foliage has a silken
spidery loveliness because its unsheathed needles grow in
tufts or tiny spray brooms." — *Idaho Writers' Project, 1950*

PLACE

In landscape photography, place is the perception of location and spatial awareness about the subject. I strive to create the sensation of place in my photographs by deciding on the best vantage point, carefully selecting the camera position and choosing a lens to give me the correct perspective. In the final composition, organization and juxtaposition of subject elements are precisely considered on the ground glass. When I achieve a sense of place in my grand landscapes, the photograph conveys the feeling that the viewer is at the edge of the frame, virtually standing in the scene.

Left: *Stanley Lake Creek spills over rocks in a Sawtooth Range gorge, Sawtooth Wilderness*

Above: *Indian rice grass at sunset, Bruneau Dunes State Park*

Overleaf: *Frosty rabbit brush and the Boulder Mountains on a crisp morning, Big Wood River Valley*

Beargrass and aspen trunks establish ground on a
talus slope, Payette Crest area in the
Salmon River Mountains

Mount Heyburn and its north arete intercept last light
in the Sawtooth Range, Sawtooth Wilderness

"The granite . . . is a coarse texture of feldspar, mica, and
quartz. This enormous rugged pavement of stone is a
geologic continuity that has intruded into innumerable
places, and unfolds, in consequence, into a panorama of
faults and gorges, corrugated ridges, black caverns, and
basaltic buttes." — *Idaho Writers' Project, 1950*

Great boulders jam Selway Falls, Selway Wild and Scenic River, Nezperce National Forest

Rabbit brush and autumn grasses surround lava boulders, Massacre Rocks State Park

"After spending parts of four months in what became Idaho, the [Lewis and Clark] expedition left, but their impact was deeply felt. They had established friendly relations with two great Indian nations, the Shoshoni and the Nez Percé. They demonstrated that a route through the northern Rockies to the Pacific Coast was difficult." — *F. Ross Peterson, 1976*

*Rainwater evaporates in granite basins at
City of Rocks, Albion Mountains*

*Yellow paintbrush accents a meadow below
McGown Peak in the Sawtooth Range,
Sawtooth National Recreation Area*

Overleaf: *Trout lilies spring forth in an aspen forest,
Henry's Lake Mountains*

"No less impressive are two cities of rock, one of them
volcanic in origin, the other of granite and calcareous
limestone shaped by wind and water and sand, and both of
them looking like an assortment of Gothic cathedrals that
have fallen into ruins." — *Idaho Writers' Project, 1950*

Wild grasses on a basalt rim overlook Big Jack's
Creek Canyon, Owyhee Plateau

Afternoon light in an aspen forest,
Pioneer Mountains

". . . the Owyhee batholith, still masked and disguised on its surface with overlapping volcanoes, or faulted and folded into an overwhelming panorama of monuments and terraces and deep river tunnels . . . is less a desert than a great natural monument of rivers bedded in stone. Besides three rivers that drain it, there are several large creeks, and all of these for the most part lie deep in their narrow sunless canyons sculptured out of rock." — *Idaho Writers' Project, 1950*

MOTION

Wind and water are the primary factors representing motion in nature's still-life world. When I'm photographing in the field, wind can be a vexatious nuisance as I struggle to arrest its attempts to blur the finer details of trees and flowers in a scene. But wind is also a manifestation of continuous change in the landscape. It can be the choreographer of clouds that become the focus of dramatic sunsets.

I also find an endless source of enchantment in the designs created by moving water. Whether tumbling through a mountain gorge or tracing around river rocks, water constantly fascinates me with its ever-changing signature of reflections and patterns.

Left: *Autumn-colored birches crowd along the South Fork Clearwater River, Clearwater Mountains*

Above: *Parker Creek finds a course around wet boulders, Selkirk Mountains, Kaniksu National Forest*

Mineral-colored water tumbles down the
Little Salmon River, Salmon River Mountains

Autumn-tinged willows line Summit Creek,
Pioneer Mountains

Overleaf: Autumn drizzle visits Thousand Springs
Fall, Snake River Gorge

". . . the overhanging verdure of the current offers exciting
possibilities for adventure, and I follow along the bank,
through thickets of alder and willow and maple, until I come
to the diminutive falls but a little way up the stream. There
. . . are rare and lacy maidenhair fern, and the delicate white
violet, and other shade-loving plants that are strange to me."
— *Nelle Portrey Davis, 1942*

---

*Autumn dogbane along the South Fork Clearwater
River, Clearwater Mountains*

*Lower Mesa Falls on the Henry's Fork,
Targhee National Forest*

"No matter which direction is taken, there will be
incalculable wonder north, east, south, and west. The path
will skirt towering mountains on which the evergreen timber
will be so dense that it will look like solid growth; past blue
lakes so numerous that nobody has ever counted them; . . .

*Waterfall on Continental Creek, Salmon-Priest area
in the Selkirk Mountains*

*Redfish Lake Creek flows below early spring
snowpack, Sawtooth National Recreation Area*

. . . through deep canyons and up high ridges from which
the streams below will look like white strings of beads; across
torrents coming in tumultuous foaming journeys down from
the moraines; through autumn gardens aflame with leaf and
with flowers smoking and fragrant under recent frosts; . . .

Autumn lines the banks of the Little Salmon River,
Salmon River Mountains

Bruneau River meanders below basalt cliffs,
Owyhee Plateau

. . . and along rocky flanks where stone, spilled in millions
of tons, defies everything but sheep and goat or the agile
mule." — *Idaho Writers' Project, 1950*

SOFT LIGHT

When photographing the intimate landscapes or details of nature, I prefer to work with soft light. The ethereal clarity of waxing twilight, the soft warm glow of morning fog, the airy tenor of bright overcast, the misty ambience of a gentle drizzle — these are my favorite conditions for nature photography.

The dramatic modeling provided by a dazzling sun is useful for characterizing the relief of landforms on a grand scale. But direct sunlight is too blunt to reveal the more subtle minutiae of a landscape. Details become cloaked in the shadows and veiled in the highlights. Only in soft light is color film able to record a full range of chromatic values and tonal information about a subject.

Left: *Beargrass romps in a spruce forest, Payette Crest area in the Salmon River Mountains*

Above: *Sunset-colored peaks in the Snake River Range rise above Palisades Reservoir, Targhee National Forest*

Moody sunset hues envelop Chimney Rock and the
Selkirk Crest, from the north arete of Mount Roothaan
in the Selkirk Mountains

Syringa, Idaho's state flower, blooms beside the
North Fork Payette River, North Fork Range

Overleaf: *Sagebrush and aspen forest on the
Continental Divide, below the Centennial Mountains*

"In any direction for a hundred miles, and in some directions
for a much greater distance than that, there is only an ocean
of thousands of zeniths, each high and imperturbable in a
misty blue integrity of its own; of thousands of lakes, each
cool and fragrant and perfect; of tens of thousands of wild
animals hiding below among the millions of trees."
— *Idaho Writers' Project, 1950*

Muted autumn colors in the Boulder Mountains,
Sawtooth National Recreation Area

Arrowleaf balsamroot and sagebrush in West Fork
Hayden Creek Canyon, Lemhi Range

"Adjacent mountains look like mounds of chalk, or like slabs of granite adorned with golden furze and tiny sub-alpine mirrors. Ranges now swim into vision, with backbones serrated in row on row, with forested depressions and altitudes stretching to the farthest reach. The enormous landscape eastward is a wilderness not only of peaks and canyons and streams, but also one of legend, . . ."
— *Idaho Writers Project, 1950*

*Western hemlocks seclude Cow Creek, Selkirk
Mountains, Kaniksu National Forest*

*Desert parsley and basalt above Big Jack's Creek
and inner gorge, Owyhee Plateau*

Overleaf: *Late afternoon light brightens the north
side of the Lost River Range and Leatherman Peak,
Challis National Forest*

"This [hemlock] tree is beautiful at any season, but it has a
special charm just as the new growth has developed at the
ends of the branches in early summer, each young twig being
of a lovely light green shade that forms a charming harmony
with the dark rich green of the rest of the branches."
— *Nelle Portrey Davis, 1942*

*Limber pine forest and relics, Norton Lakes basin in
the Smoky Mountains*

*Little penstemons invade an avalanche slide area in
the Sawtooth Range, Sawtooth Wilderness*

"The clear, deep tone of the mountain bluebirds made gay
notes of color against the somber woods. The warmth of the
morning brought out the pungent fragrance of the pines.
The timber breeze was clean and fresh and springlike, but
it reminded one a bit of winter, too, as though remembering
the little patches of needle-strewn snow but lately gone from
the fastnesses of the deep woods." — *Nelle Portrey Davis, 1942*

MICROCOSM &
MACROCOSM

In nature photography, microcosm and macrocosm represent the diametrical extremes of scale in our visual world. On one hand we have the world of macrocosm, the vastness of sweeping panoramas and immense scale. It is the realm of infinite distances and the perception of open space. On the other hand, the world of microcosm is the miniature scene at our feet or suddenly before our faces. This is the realm of curious details and bizarre patterns that we see when we inspect everyday nature more closely. By employing the camera to see for us, it is possible to augment our vision of the natural world.

Left: *Ponderosa pine needles on a bed of club moss, Salmon River Mountains*

Above: *Castle Peak overlooks Chamberlain Basin in the White Cloud Peaks, Sawtooth National Recreation Area*

Desert parsley blooms on fractured pahoehoe lava,
Craters of the Moon National Monument

Mountain death camas blooms profusely in a
montane meadow, Bitterroot Range

"Southward the eruptive volcanic rocks lie in superimposed
flows, including the basaltic sculpturings in the Craters of
the Moon . . . a rolling mass of loneliness and waste, with
the integrity of granite and the changelessness of time."
— *F. Ross Peterson, 1976*

Rabbit brush and hare tracks in new snow,
Snake River Plain

Dried plants punctuate the surface of a pahoehoe lava
flow, Craters of the Moon National Monument

Overleaf: *Sunset pastels paint Lake Pend Oreille,*
below the Cabinet Mountains

" . . . it is a splendid and timeless area upon which a thousand
centuries will leave almost no mark of change . . . its caves
and craters and the weird terracing of its scene. . . . looking
as if the sky had poured boulders upon it or as if it harbored
a vegetation of rock; . . . This is the last frontier, delivered
to rock and desolation and set apart as a monument of its
own." — *F. Ross Peterson, 1976*

*Ice forms around stones in the Salmon River at
10 degrees below zero, Pahsimeroi Mountains*

*Beads of morning dew cling to lupines,
Bitterroot Range*

Overleaf: *Devils Bedstead and sunset clouds above
Kane Creek Canyon, Pioneer Mountains*

"The dainty twin bells and the showy Indian paintbrush are
other spring flowers that like to get the important business
of blooming out of the way before the dryer season of early
summer comes along. But the purple daisies, the meadow
lilies and the lupines await the more barren season of
mid-summer to flaunt their welcome colors."
— *Nelle Portrey Davis, 1942*

*Afternoon shadows envelop Alice Lake in the
Sawtooth Range, Sawtooth Wilderness*

*Bunchberry and False Solomon's seal cover the forest
floor, Bitterroot Range, Selway-Bitterroot Wilderness*

"The effect on the human intruder of the cold clean air, the open azure
sky, and the green-carpeted mountains below is overcoming, and a
powerful euphoria almost sweeps one from the high and lofty perches.
It is just as overwhelming to lie prone upon a small windy mountain
trail and sip at the icy clear water trickling from a spring and realize
that within a few miles the water that seeps from the hillside will be
cascading creek, then a raging river, . . . Another emotional experience
is to walk quietly upon needle carpet through the majestic white pine
forests of northern Idaho and recall that some of these towering pines
stood when Lewis and Clark . . . passed by. This great natural legacy
stands as a beacon to the nation." — *F. Ross Peterson, 1976*

TECHNICAL
INFORMATION

The photographic images for this book were made with Toyo 4x5 and 8x10 field view cameras and focused with Nikkor and Fujinon lenses ranging from 65mm to 600mm.

Exposures were calculated with a Pentax 1-degree spot meter and sometimes supplemented with averaging and incident light readings taken with a Gossen Luna Pro SBC. Warming filters were occasionally used to correct the color cast in deep shade. Lens apertures ranged from f/16 to f/64, and shutter speeds varied between 1/8th of a second and 20 seconds.

Ektachrome and Fujichrome professional daylight transparency films were used to record the images.

Folded limestone cliffs on Mount Breitenbach loom over the East Fork Pahsimeroi River Valley, Lost River Range